Equal Access
Fighting for Disability Protections™

Adaptive Sports and the Paralympic Games

Barbara Gottfried

Rosen
YA™
New York

To my son Raffi ("Richard"), who shows me the true meaning of "I CAN." I am so proud to be your mother.

Published in 2020 by The Rosen Publishing Group, Inc.
29 East 21st Street, New York, NY 10010

Library of Congress Cataloging-in-Publication Data

Names: Gottfried, Barbara author.
Title: Adaptive sports and the Paralympic Games / Barbara Gottfried.
Description: First edition. | New York : Rosen YA, 2020 | Series: Equal access: fighting for disability protections | Includes bibliographical references and index. | Audience: Grades: 7–12.
Identifiers: LCCN 2018010908| ISBN 9781508183310 (library bound) | ISBN 9781508183303 (paperback)
Subjects: LCSH: Paralympics—Juvenile literature. | Sports for people with disabilities—Juvenile literature.
Classification: LCC GV722.5.P37 G67 2019 | DDC 796.087/4—dc23
LC record available at https://lccn.loc.gov/2018010908

Manufactured in the United States of America

The editors of this resource have consulted various organizations' style guides, including that of the National Center on Disability and Journalism, to ensure the language herein is accurate, sensitive, and respectful. In accordance with NCDJ's recommendation, we have deferred to our author's preference of either people-first or identity-first language.

Table of Contents

Introduction...................... 4

Chapter One
Ability to be Active 8

Chapter Two
Sports While Seated.............. 19

Chapter Three
Water Sports..................... 29

Chapter Four
Snow Sports...................... 37

Chapter Five
So Many Choices.................. 46

Glossary......................... 54
For More Information............. 56
For Further Reading.............. 58
Bibliography..................... 59
Index............................ 62

Introduction

Exercise, including training for athletic competitions, provides physical, emotional, and social benefits. Different parts of the body—like the brain and muscles—stay healthier with regular exercise. Hormones released during exercise help people feel happier. And many sports-related activities involving others—from coaches to teammates—provide opportunities for social interaction.

But what about the millions of people whose disabilities prevent them from engaging in traditional physical activities? These may be people with physical impairments—such as amputees, who lost part or all of their limbs, or those with severe cerebral palsy. What about those with Down syndrome or autism spectrum disorders? Shouldn't everyone be able to gain the benefits of exercise?

In the last few decades, the United States has passed federal laws, like the Americans with Disabilities Act (ADA), to ensure that people with disabilities have the same rights as others, in school, the workplace, and other public or private places. One of the things these laws are meant to protect is the ability of people with disabilities to participate in physical activities, often with modifications, including having access to sports-related buildings by providing wheelchair ramps and elevators.

People of all abilities enjoy the physical and mental health benefits of regular exercise. Innovations, including prosthetics as replacements for limbs, allow amputees to engage in exercise.

Today, there are many options for people with disabilities to compete in sports such as skiing, volleyball, basketball, or table tennis, whether in games with classmates in school or in international competitions. Adaptive sports, also known as para sports, are recreational or competitive sports for people with disabilities. They allow people with physical or intellectual impairments to engage in physical activities by modifying the activity, equipment, or both.

Both the Paralympics and the Special Olympics provide opportunities for athletes with physical and intellectual impairments to compete in different adaptive sports with their peers from around the world. While the Special Olympics focuses primarily on athletes with intellectual disabilities, the Paralympics offers almost thirty sports for athletes with physical disabilities and runs parallel to the traditional Olympics. The "para-" in Paralympics refers to parallel—which means "equal to"—because these games occur in the same place as the traditional Olympics, immediately following that competition.

In 1960, the Paralympics first debuted with four hundred athletes from twenty-three countries. The first modern summer Paralympic Games were held in South Korea in 1988, with opening ceremonies that included thousands of children and seven hundred wheelchair dancers. Today, the number of Paralympic sports keeps growing, with surfing a possible addition for the 2024 Paris Paralympic Games.

These young athletes received medals after participating in a Special Olympics event in Florida. The Special Olympics gives individuals with intellectual disabilities the chance to compete in a wide range of sports.

As Jack Rutter, Paralympic football competitor from the United Kingdom, shared in a 2016 Huffington Post article, "I try and show everyone what can happen if you overcome adversity and keep trying to do the right things. Stick to some key skills: honesty, respect, determination—and eventually you'll be able to achieve your dreams."

Chapter One

Ability to be Active

According to surveys from the Centers for Disease Control and Prevention (CDC), 28.4 percent of people with disabilities report being in excellent or very good health—compared to 61.4 percent of those without disabilities. What can promote good health? People of all abilities benefit from being active. Both recreational and competitive exercise helps people lead longer, healthier, and more productive lives. Adaptive sports organizations, like the Paralympics, offer opportunities to take exercise to a highly competitive level. In *The Super-Human Olympics: The Paralympics* by Mamta Jaswal, Joey Reiman, an educator, businessman, and writer who once had partial paralysis, states, "What I learned was that these athletes were not disabled, they were super-abled. The Olympics is where heroes are made. The Paralympics is where heroes come."

The Benefits of Exercise

Being active has physical health benefits. The body has several systems that work together to help it function properly:

Nervous system: Comprised of the brain, spinal cord, and nerves, the nervous system controls all other systems.

Skeletal and muscular system: Made up of the bones and muscles, the skeletal and muscular system protects the nervous system and heart, lungs, and kidneys and helps people move.

Digestive system: Starting in the mouth and then moving down to the stomach and intestines, the digestive system turns food into energy for the body.

Respiratory system: Made up of the nose, larynx, trachea, and lungs, among other organs, the respiratory system takes in oxygen for the body.

Circulatory system: Made up of the heart and blood vessels, the circulatory system moves oxygen throughout the body and moves waste.

Urinary system: Made up of the kidneys and bladder as well as the ureters and urethra, the urinary system cleans blood from the body and gets rid of waste products that are not needed by cells.

Exercise helps these systems work together better. For example, consider a swimmer. Her heart beats faster to pump blood to her muscles. She experiences an increase in the flow of oxygen. Both the extra blood and oxygen are good for her brain! They make the swimmer more alert and focused and even release hormones, called endorphins, which make her feel happy. This type of reaction happens with other forms of exercise, too.

Exercise also affects the heart of a person doing aerobic exercise. The amount of blood flowing and returning to the heart increases. This increase causes a part of the heart, called the left ventricle, to become bigger. The heart is now capable of holding even more blood and ejecting more blood with each beat. The result is a drop in the resting heart rate, which makes it easier for the heart to function. Exercise also lowers the pressure of blood in the circulatory system. High blood pressure is a major risk factor for heart disease. The best kinds of exercise to lower blood pressure include walking, jogging, swimming, and cycling.

Exercise helps people's bodies in other ways, too. The muscular system is responsible for how the body moves. Exercise strengthens muscles. For a person in a wheelchair who uses his arms to help with transports, exercises that strengthen his arm muscles will make for easier transports—both for himself and his personal care assistants.

Down syndrome is a chromosomal disorder with traits such as low muscle tone, an upward eye slant, a short attention span, and impulsive behavior.

Preexercise stretching also helps people develop better balance and coordination and improve posture. Stretching loosens and warms up muscles, which is especially helpful for disabled people with hypertonia, or excessive muscle tone.

Although some physical diseases are more often found in the elderly, people of all ages are at risk for certain conditions, such as diabetes, heart disease, and strokes. Regular exercise, including training for physical competitions, decreases the risk of getting these illnesses. Osteoporosis is a bone disease that is more often found in older people. But it is also prevalent in another group— people who are nonambulatory, or unable to walk. Women with Down syndrome are also at higher risk

Federal Laws that Protect Students with Disabilities

In the United States, several major federal laws accommodate students with disabilities. The 2004 Individuals with Disabilities Education Act (IDEA) requires that schools meet the educational needs of students with disabilities, including providing physical education services. IDEA provides funding for the needed services and encourages parent participation in the process.

(continued on the next page)

(continued from the previous page)

Section 504 of the Rehabilitation Act of 1973 was the first civil rights law that prohibited discrimination against people with disabilities in programs receiving federal financial assistance. Regulations of Section 504, along with the IDEA, further state that each qualified student with a disability—no matter how severe—is entitled to a free appropriate public education (FAPE).

The Americans with Disabilities Act of 1990 (ADA) prohibits discrimination against people with disabilities in all public areas, like schools, workplaces, and transportation. It also applies to public and private places open to the public, such as hotels and restaurants.

for osteoporosis, perhaps due to lower peak bone density levels, which is a measure of bone strength.

Emotional and Social Wellness

Regular exercise improves a person's mental state. It promotes healthy changes in the brain, like new brain patterns, reduction of inflammation, and neural growth in a part of the brain called the hippocampus, linked to learning and memory. And exercise releases endorphins, or neurotransmitters associated with feeling happy.

Exercise also relieves stress, helps people sleep better, breaks challenging emotional cycles, and improves memory and attention spans. These effects can help people suffering from mental and learning disorders, such as depression, anxiety, and attention deficit hyperactivity disorder (ADHD). For example, aside from endorphins, exercise can also boost the hormones dopamine and serotonin, which affect focus and attention.

Exercise can make people of all abilities feel stronger, both physically and emotionally, since our bodies and minds work together. Reaching an exer-

Athletes with disabilities can enjoy team sports just as much as their peers without disabilities. Beyond the physical and emotional benefits, there is a sense of belonging that comes from being part of a team.

cise goal, like a milestone for competition training, can contribute to a sense of accomplishment and boost self-esteem. Regular exercise can also boost the immune system, helping you stay healthy. You may choose to exercise individually or be part of

Fight for Your Rights: ADA in Action

Casey Martin, who has a circulatory disorder that causes extreme weakness in his right leg, could not initially play in certain golf tournaments because the Professional Golfers' Association (PGA) did not allow a cart modification. He sued under the ADA calling the PGA Tour a "public accommodation" and Martin won the right to play. In an article titled "Faces of the ADA" on the ADA website (www.ada.gov), Martin shares, "Without the ADA I never would have been able to pursue my dream of playing golf professionally."

The ADA also seeks to make buildings—including sports facilities—accessible for all. Michael Sack, who has cerebral palsy, stated in an article "Personal Stories of the ADA's Impact" on Minnesota Public Radio that "sports facilities have become ADA approved, including Target Field and TCF Bank Stadium. Yes, I have been affected by the passing of the ADA."

US golfer Casey Martin, who was born with a circulatory disorder that causes pain and leg swelling, won a Supreme Court case that allowed him to use a golf cart when competing in golf tournaments.

a team. Exercise through team sports can foster communication, build friendships, promote social awareness, and create fun experiences. In short, exercise is good for you!

Adaptive Sports Organizations

Exercise—from leisurely walks to training for competitions—has both physical and mental benefits. Everyone should be able to participate in something that makes you feel good. People with disabilities can engage in a category of recreational or competitive sports called adaptive sports. These involve using modifications, like ski equipment for people who regularly use wheelchairs or sighted guides for

15

In the 2016 Rio de Janeiro Paralympics, Japan's Shinya Wada advanced to the final, competing with an escort runner in the visually impaired 500-meter race.

visually impaired runners. Some adaptive sport classifications for competitions also use guidelines to group athletes of similar abilities together.

The Paralympics and the Special Olympics are two separate organizations that include adaptive sports. Both are recognized by the International Olympic Committee (IOC) and are run by international nonprofit groups, but the organizations are different in three main ways. First, the Paralympics include athletes in six categories: (1) those with cerebral palsy, (2) amputees, (3) those with spinal injuries, (4) the visually impaired, (5) the intellectually impaired, and (6) others (known as "Les Autres"). The Special Olympics focuses on (1) those with intellectual disabilities, (2) cognitive delays, (3) developmental delays, and (4) physical delays. The Paralympics tends to include athletes with more physical disabilities, while the Special Olympics focuses on those with intellectual disabilities.

Another difference is that the Paralympics is a competition with strict criteria and standards that must be met to compete, while the Special Olympics encourages everyone to participate and does not exclude anyone based on qualifying scores.

The two organizations also differ greatly in structure. The Paralympics is an international sports representative organization that provides a very competitive forum for athletes with disabilities; while the Special Olympics is a global movement aimed at building a worldwide network of athletes and fostering an environment of inclusion, acceptance, and dignity for people of all abilities.

To compete in the Special Olympics, an athlete must be at least eight years old. The Paralympics, as stipulated through the International Paralympics Committee, does not have a minimum age requirement to compete, but individual Paralympic sports may have separate requirements. Track and field has a minimum age of fourteen, for example.

Being able to compete in adaptive sports programs gives people with disabilities many of the same opportunities already given to those without disabilities. It also allows an important part of the population—those with intellectual and physical challenges—to break down societal barriers, like negative attitudes and discrimination. As Hilary Beeton, an occupational therapist and an International Paralympic Committee's classifier, who determines which classification is appropriate for each athlete, stated, "Sports provides a platform for acquiring life skills."

Myths & Facts

Myth: Exercise has only physical benefits.

Fact: Exercise, including team sports, also has mental and social benefits, such as increasing feelings of happiness, boosting self-esteem, and promoting friendships.

Myth: People with disabilities cannot compete in sports competitions.

Fact: Organizations offering adaptive sports, like the Paralympics and Special Olympics, provide opportunities for people of different physical and intellectual abilities to compete in more than thirty different sports.

Myth: Laws cannot help people with disabilities who want to participate in sports.

Fact: Federal laws, like the 2004 Individuals with Disabilities Education Act (IDEA) and the Americans with Disabilities Act (ADA), give people with disabilities access to athletic programs. These laws also make many sports-related locations, like arenas, more accessible.

Chapter Two

Sports While Seated

As of December 2016, 2.2 million people in the United States relied on a wheelchair for daily tasks and mobility. Another 6.5 million people use assistive devices, like canes, walkers, and crutches to perform these functions. Millions of people need assistance to move, including to participate in sports. Wheelchair sports offer the accommodations necessary for millions of people to receive the physical and mental benefits of exercise. The Paralympics offers opportunities for people with disabilities to engage in intense international competitions for sports, including basketball, sitting volleyball, running, tennis, and fencing.

Hoops for All

For those in wheelchairs who are interested in shooting hoops, the Paralympics offers wheelchair basketball. This sport, governed by the International Wheelchair Basketball Federation, is played on a court of approximately the same dimensions as an NBA court (28 meters [31 yards] by 15 meters [16 yards]). Other aspects of the game,

In the 2016 Rio de Janeiro Paralympics, Canada and Argentina competed against each other in women's wheelchair basketball. The United States won the gold medal in this event.

including basket height (10 feet [3 meters]), playing time (four ten-minute quarters), twenty-four-second shot clock, three-point line, and scoring (one, two, and three-point shots) are the same as regular basketball.

Each team has five players on the court at a time. Dribbling consists of a player taking one or two pushes with the ball in her hand or lap. After the push, the player must dribble the ball with the pattern continuing. If the player pushes more than twice without the dribble, it's a travel violation. The wheelchair is also considered part of the player, so any illegal personal contact can come from touching the player or the chair.

The sport was invented around 1945 as part of a rehabilitation program for injured World War II veterans. As a Paralympic sport, wheelchair basketball debuted in 1960, with the United States and Israel strongest in the sport. At the 2016 Paralympics, twelve men's teams and ten women's teams competed. Wheelchair basketball can be found in more than one hundred countries. Some colleges and community centers throughout the United States also offer wheelchair basketball opportunities at different levels.

The Role of Disabled Veterans in Adaptive Sports

How did adaptive sports become widely introduced? After World War II, people wanted to help war veterans and civilians injured in the war. In 1944, a spinal injuries center was opened at Great Britain's Stoke Mandeville Hospital, which included rehabilitation sports. Dr. Ludwig Guttman, who opened the center, also organized wheelchair athlete competitions that coincided with the 1948 opening ceremony of the Olympic Games in London.

What began as the International Stoke Mandeville Games later became known as the Paralympic Games. In 1960, the first Paralympics took place in Italy, where four hundred athletes from twenty-three countries competed. Over the years, the Paralympics has grown. In the 2018 Paralympic Winter Games in Pyeongchang, 567 athletes competed. Team USA finished on top in the overall medal count, winning thirty-six medals. Military veterans captured eight medals

(continued on the next page)

(continued from the previous page)

overall, with six of them earned by members of the gold medal winning men's sled hockey team.

During the 2014 National Veterans Wheelchair Games, athlete Tammy Landeen competed in the slalom course, which involved moving through obstacles quickly under the guidance of staff and volunteers.

Sitting Volleyball

Volleyball is all about cooperation, power, and, of course, hitting the ball over the net. Standing and sitting volleyball have many similarities, but they also have some important differences. Those participating in sitting volleyball are seated with their pelvises in contact with the floor at all times. Because of the athlete's positions, the net is lower than the standing volleyball version (1.15 meters [3.8 feet] for men and 1.05 meters [3.4 feet] for women), with court dimensions also being smaller (10 meters [33 feet] by 6 meters [20 feet]).

Teams get three passes before the ball must go over the net. The winning team is the first to reach twenty-five points, with a minimum of a two-point lead, in the best of five games. Many athletes who play sitting volleyball are amputees, who have lost all or part of a limb, like an arm or leg. While standing volleyball originated in Holyoke, Massachusetts, sitting volleyball came from the Netherlands. It found its way into the 1976 Toronto Paralympics and is played in about sixty countries today.

Barriers to Inclusion in Sport

People with disabilities often face challenges when trying to be included in mainstream sports activities. These challenges can come from different places. For example, people without disabilities may not know how to include everyone in sports-related activities. Or programs with adaptive sports options may not exist in certain areas. Often, facilities that are not wheelchair accessible, without ramps or elevators, also pose physical barriers for inclusion.

Increasing inclusion can be done in several ways, including:

- Providing programs for those with disabilities at different times from mainstream programs.
- Offering parallel activities with different populations doing the same activity in different ways.

(continued on the next page)

(continued from the previous page)

- Including people with and without disabilities in activities designed for those with disabilities.
- Being more flexible on how activities are done—like unstructured movement games in which people can participate in their own ways.

More Than One Way to Run

Competitive running means going from a starting point to an ending point. But there are different ways of reaching your destination. Some people with disabilities have prostheses—artificial body parts, such as legs, that allow them to participate in sports like running. Others have racing chairs that help athletes with disabilities reach the finish line faster. Running guides are another option for those with visual impairments.

Once people decide on the preferred mode to run, they need to figure out their goals. How far to run? What speed to go? How many days to commit to running? Initial goals may differ a lot from final ones. A runner may begin with a shorter distance in more time but eventually work up to greater distances with consistently short times per mile.

Having a goal—like a 5k race, marathon, or Paralympic qualifying event—can also help runners stick to their running regimen. Marathons in several US cities, such as Boston, Chicago, Detroit, Los

Angeles, and New York, offer options for the visually impaired or the mobility impaired—like push-rim
wheelchairs. While the average wheelchair user
pushes two thousand to three thousand times per
day, creating wear and tear on their hands and
wrists, push-rim chairs increase pushing power and
alleviate the strain on upper limbs. Having a coach
and realistic expectations also help athletes reach
their goals.

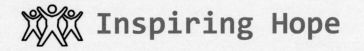 Inspiring Hope

In 1962, Rick Hoyt was born with spastic cerebral
palsy. This condition also meant he had quadriple-
gia, meaning he cannot control his limbs. At that
time, many of today's opportunities for people with
disabilities did not exist. But Rick's parents, Dick
and Judy, were determined to provide their son with
many of the same rights available to those without
disabilities—like an education, a way to communi-
cate, and inclusion in sports activities. For years,
they fought for people to see beyond Rick's physical disabilities, even working with a group of
engineers at Tufts University to develop a communication device that allowed Rick to cheer for his

(continued on the next page)

25

(continued from the previous page)

favorite local Boston sports teams! Finally, at the age of thirteen, Rick was admitted to public school and went on to receive a degree in special education from Boston University.

An event in 1977 changed the lives of the Hoyts and so many other people. Rick, who uses a wheelchair, wanted to participate in a 5-mile (8 km) run to help a local lacrosse player who had become paralyzed from an accident. Dick decided to push Rick in his wheelchair to the finish line. After the race, Rick said, "Dad, when I'm running, it feels like I'm not handicapped." This was the beginning of Team Hoyt and its foundation. Over the next few decades, father and son would run more than one thousand races together, including marathons, duathlons, and triathlons—six of these were Ironman competitions. And that's not all! In 1992, they also ran and biked a total of 3,735 miles (6,011 kilometers) in forty-five days together—inspiring people around the world and making the seemingly impossible possible.

In 2015, Rick Hoyt, who was paralyzed at birth, took part in the Boston Marathon, his thirty-third, with the help of friend Bryan Lyons.

Accommodations Make the Difference

Wheelchair tennis is one of the fastest-growing wheelchair sports. Like basketball and volleyball, it requires and builds a lot of upper body strength. Much of this sport is the same as the standing version, including court size and equipment, such as rackets and balls. But there are two main differences: players use wheelchairs and the balls can bounce up to two times. This sport debuted in the 1992 Paralympics.

Abilities Expos, like the one shown above, take place throughout the country. These exhibitions provide people with disabilities the opportunity to learn about products designed to improve their quality of life.

People with leg and feet impairments, like amputations and spinal-cord injuries, can also try wheelchair fencing. Fencing is a sport that includes athletes using swords, such as foils, épées, or sabers, and strategy to score points. Wheelchair fencing competition includes wheelchairs being anchored to the ground. Athletes then fence without moving their chairs in an area about 4 meters (13.1 feet) by 1.5 meters (4.9 feet). Special sensors determine what is a valid point.

In the Paralympics, fencing athletes are also categorized by abilities of the arm and trunk, or the central part of the body from which the limbs and the head extend. For example, one category has athletes with good trunk control; while another category includes people with impaired trunks or fencing arms. Teens wanting to participate in wheelchair fencing can look for adaptive training programs in their local areas or inquire at Abilities Expos, a place for people with disabilities, their caregivers, and health care professionals to come together to share products and services.

Chapter Three

Water Sports

Water decreases a person's weight by 90 percent. Being in the water allows people to move without putting too much stress on the skeletal and muscular system. In fact, aqua therapy helps many people with disabilities, like those with severe cerebral palsy, improve their physical functioning by reducing muscle and joint pain, improving muscle tone, enhancing circulation, improving flexibility, and extending their range of motion. The Paralympics offers adaptive competitions in swimming, water skiing, sailing, and paddle sports such as canoeing, kayaking, rowing, and rafting.

Ways to Paddle

For people with physical or intellectual impairments, paddle sports require modifications to equipment, coaching, and program structure. People who participate in adaptive rowing may have autism, amputations, visual impairment, paraplegia (paralysis of legs and lower body), cerebral palsy, Down syndrome, spina bifida, or other conditions resulting in a disability.

Juan Carlos Gil, who has cerebral palsy and is legally blind, participates in adaptive rowing at the Miami Beach Rowing Club in Miami Beach, Florida.

The kind of adaptations needed depend on both the person and the sport. For example, a person with severe cerebral palsy can use a kayak or canoe mount to help with head support, spinal alignment, and pelvic stability. These mounts, which are like seat inserts, use clamps to mount to the flat bench seats. The mounts are intended to provide lateral stability, which is the ability to regain or keep one's original position by using forces or having them imposed. The paddler may also require a transfer board, positioned at wheelchair height and located directly above the kayak's seat. A transfer board is a device that bridges the space between the wheelchair and another place, like a bed, toilet, car seat…or kayak!

The Paralympics has four classifications for athletes participating in para rowing, which is determined based on several tests and a medical evaluation. For example, the legs, trunk, arms (LTA) class may include rowers with an amputation, neurological impairment, cerebral palsy, or visual impairment who can support themselves on the sliding seat. These athletes use their legs, trunk, and arms to make the boat go faster. A test for this classification may be doing a full squat and then   coming back to a full standing position.

In the Water

The Paralympics has been offering competitions in swimming since the games began in 1960. Athletes are grouped according to physical, visual, or intellectual impairment. For example, there are ten physical

During the 2016 Rio de Janeiro Paralympics, twenty-four-year-old American swimmer Jessica Long won a silver medal in the Women's 400m Freestyle S8.

impairment classifications, ranging from the loss of one hand or a movement limitation in one hip joint to significant loss of muscle power or control in the limbs, which requires a wheelchair for daily life. No prostheses or assistive devices are allowed in the water.

Para-swimming athletes arc tested in freestyle, backstroke, butterfly, breaststroke, and medley. Modifications can be made, such as beginning the race in the water instead of on a starting platform or having an assistant called a tapper help swimmers with visual impairments know when the pool end wall is approaching. In the Rio 2016 Paralympic Games, twenty-five-year-old swimmer Jessica Long took home gold, silver, and bronze medals and became the second-most-decorated Paralympian in US history.

Ellie Simmonds Wins Gold

Ellie Simmonds has achondroplasia, which is a common cause of dwarfism. This Paralympian won her first gold medal at the age of thirteen, in para swimming. Simmonds was the youngest British athlete at the 2008 Beijing Paralympics, but that did not stop her from taking home gold medals in both the 100-meter and 400-meter freestyle competitions. After the 2016 Rio Paralympics, Simmonds's medal total was up to eight Paralympic medals, including five gold.

How did her home country of England respond? Simmonds was named a Member of the Order of the British Empire (MBE) by the queen in 2009. She was the youngest person to receive the MBE. Simmonds was also named an Officer of the Order of the British Empire (OBE) in 2013 for her Paralympic participation.

Simmonds is the youngest of five children and her sister Katie also has achondroplasia. In a *Guardian* article, Simmonds shared:

> I've always been aware of being shorter, but I felt as if I could do anything. I don't remember my mum and dad telling me anything and they certainly didn't make any special allowances for Katie and me. They said if I wanted to achieve something I shouldn't let it stop me.

Sailing Around the World

In the 1980s, Switzerland hosted the first international sailing competition for athletes with disabilities. In 1988, the International Handicap Sailing Committee (IHSC) was created; and by 1990, the sport debuted at the World Games for the Disabled. In 2000, sailing found its way to the Paralympics, with two events—the single-person and three-person keelboat. A keelboat has a weighted keel that keeps it from turning over, or capsizing, and it's larger and more stable than a boat called a dinghy.

Getting in and out of the boat can be difficult for some people with disabilities, requiring mechanical lifts, transfer boarding benches, and personal assistants. Adaptations for people with disabilities also include special seating for better support, electric starter motors that begin the engine's operation, and a talking GPS. Many of the tools modify or perform manual operations, like controlling the sail and the rudder. If you're interested, look online for adaptive sailing programs that meet your needs, and as Bob Ewing, president of Seattle's

The C. Thomas Clagett, Jr. Memorial Clinic & Regatta is the top event for sailors with disabilities, often providing training for the Paralympics.

Footloose Sailing Association, said in a 2017 *Seattle Times* article, "Leave your disability at the dock."

Water Skiing, Anyone?

For a person who needs to sit while water skiing, sit skis come in beginner, intermediate/advanced, jump, and trick versions. The beginner skis are wider with a starting block, or raised platform, that holds the rope for those having difficulty gripping things. These skis are also more stable than the others because of their shape and depth. The intermediate/advanced ski does not usually have a starting block and comes with modifications for competition, such as edge designs that help athletes ski better. Jump skis are built to use for competitions involving jumping; while trick skis are made for moves like 360-degree spins.

In addition to ski types, the jump and trick are also two kinds of competition categories. The jump involves going over a ramp with height options varying from 1 meter (3.3 ft) to 1.5 meters (4.9 ft) and set width and length. The trick involves an athlete doing

Houston-based Texas Adaptive Aquatics provides an opportunity for more than fifty adults and children with disabilities to water ski.

Interview with Adam Combs, Cofounder and Codirector of Waypoint Adventure

Waypoint Adventure is a nonprofit educational organization that uses quality experiential and adventure-based programs. According to its website, "The mission of Waypoint Adventure is to challenge youth and adults with disabilities to discover their purpose, talents, and strengths through the transforming power of adventure." Waypoint Adventure offers adaptive outdoor activities, like kayaking, rope courses, rock climbing, day hikes, zip lining, and snowshoeing.

Question: What is an outdoor adventure program at Waypoint?

Adam: Outdoor adventure is made up of adventurous challenges and outdoor activities…These activities push us to challenge ourselves physically, emotionally, and socially in ways that we might not otherwise… It's a great way to strengthen the bonds that you might already have with friends and family or meet new friends!

Question: How are Waypoint's activities accessible?

Adam: We work hard to make sure that all of our programs are fully accessible to people with a wide range of disabilities. Waypoint brings

(continued on the next page)

(continued from the previous page)

together three things to provide support — community, access, preparation. We call this our "CAP Sauce" recipe for support...Customized curriculum and adaptive equipment create the "access" at Waypoint.

Question: What is one of your favorite Waypoint moments?

Adam: It happened in the summer of 2016 on a [full day] kayaking program just outside of Boston with a twenty-six-year-old young lady who has cerebral palsy and is a full-time power wheelchair user...It was a very windy day. The young lady and her boat partner had had a really difficult time maneuvering their kayak all day...As I paddled past them, the young lady looked at me and said, 'you know, I need to do this more often...with my disability, my life isn't always easy. Sometimes it's hard to get up and get dressed. Sometimes it's hard to get in and out of my wheelchair or in and out of buildings. Doing things like this reminds me that I can. If I can finish this trip, I can do anything!'

two twenty-second passes with as many tricks as possible and none done more than once. The wakeboard competition is like the trick competition but uses a different ski and is more about the air tricks. The slalom contest is an 800-foot (244 m) course around buoys at potentially increased speeds.

Chapter Four

Snow Sports

For those living in areas with snow-filled winters or those wanting to try cold-weather sports, adaptive sports include cross-country skiing, downhill skiing, sled hockey, snowboarding, and curling. Modifications make these sports accessible for those with physical and intellectual impairments. An exhibit at the Smithsonian's National Museum of American History called *Everyone Plays! Sports and Disabilities* highlighted some of these historical modifications—like the precursor to the sit ski, called the mono ski, adaptive athlete Buddy Elias's snowboard with crutch rig that allowed him to ski after his leg was amputated, and paraplegic Chris Douglas's hockey sled that he used to compete on the US National Sled Hockey Team.

Hitting the Slopes

States from California to New Hampshire, as well as the Canadian provinces, offer adaptive ski programs. Doing an online search can help you locate the programs in your area. Some programs are only for adaptive sports and others are mainstream ski programs that offer modifications. Cross-country skiing involves traveling over snow on a mix of terrains; while downhill skiers enjoy the thrill of going down mountains of snow at fast speeds.

The kind of equipment a person needs depends on his disability. Two-track skiing is for athletes who can stand on two legs and maintain balance while moving, such as skiers with developmental, cognitive, visual, or hearing impairments including mild cerebral palsy, Asperger's syndrome, and Fragile X syndrome. A skier who must sit-ski can try a mono-ski or bi-ski. The mono-ski includes a bucket seat

Both the Paralympics and the Special Olympics offer adaptive cross-country skiing. The Special Olympics offers four snow sports: cross-country skiing, alpine skiing, snowboarding, and snowshoeing.

with one ski underneath; while the bi-ski has two skis under the bucket seat.

Which seat is right for you? If you have good trunk balance, strong arms, and solid core strength, then try mono-skiing, which uses handheld out-riggers, or a framework that acts as a support. If you are usually in a wheelchair or need an assis-tive device to walk, then try bi-skiing. A person can bi-ski by holding outriggers or by having an instruc-tor hold the support.

Options for adaptive skiing exist for people with disabilities beginning at a young age. For exam-ple, ski carts enable people with severe disabilities to participate. These carts have molded fiberglass shells connected to a metal chassis and resting on four skis. Skiers can turn the carts' front wheels using controls presented at waist level; or instruc-tors can control the cart using a tether rope. Another opportunity called Nordic Rocks for Schools program provides students from kindergarten to sixth grade with sit-ski equipment for Nordic skiing.

Nordic and Alpine skiing are the two kinds of competitive skiing. Nordic includes cross-country, jumping, and biathlon; while Alpine consists of downhill and slalom racing, which includes going around markers. Skiers can compete in differ-ent classes. For example, Sport Classes LW 2-9: Standing Skiers includes skiers with leg or arm impairments or both; while Class LW 10-12 is for sit-skiers and Class B1-3 is for skiers with visual impairments. In 1980, downhill racing debuted at the Paralympics in Norway, while mono-skiing was introduced in the 1988 Innsbruck Games.

American Stephen Lawler competed in the Men's Giant Slalom Sitting in the 2001 Paralympic Games in Christchurch, New Zealand, and the 2018 games in Pyeongchang, South Korea.

Let's Sledge

Adaptive sled hockey, also known as sledge outside the United States, surfaced in Sweden at a physical rehabilitation center in the early 1960s. If you're familiar with the rules of typical ice hockey, you can understand sledge. Each team has six players: three forwards, two players on defense, and one goalie. Each period is twenty minutes, takes place on an ice rink, and the goal is to score by getting the puck into the net.

What's the difference between sled hockey and stand-up hockey? The equipment! People playing sled hockey participate in sleds that sit on top of two hockey skate blades so pucks can pass underneath.

40

Teen Joins 2018 US Paralympic Nordic Ski Team

Inspired by athletes who skied with one arm in a race based in Canada, Alaskan Grace Miller took to the slopes. By eighteen, Grace Miller was a member of the US Nordic Ski Team headed to the Paralympics in Pyeongchang, South Korea. In an *Anchorage Daily News* article, Miller shared, the "first time I had ever seen anybody else ski with one pole and with one hand [at the World Cup in Canada], it was just amazing."

Born in China and brought to the United States at the age of three by her adopted mother, Miller began skiing at four years old. She skied with a team located in Eagle River in middle school and then the Palmer High School Ski Team. On February 1, 2018, Miller received word that she had been chosen to represent the United States at the Paralympic Games in March. Miller was surprised to be selected for Team USA. While training can be hard work, Miller shared, "Kids on the ski team usually have similar interests so it's really easy to make friends. It's really nice to have someone to train with or go mess around on skis, it's really fun."

In sledge hockey, metal frame with two blades underneath allows the puck to pass underneath, allowing the players to score a goal.

The players hold two sticks, instead of one, with metal picks at the end, and the goalies have special gloves. Many people can play sled hockey, including amputees, those with spinal cord injuries, and spina bifida. On disabledsportsUSA.org, Tom Carr, assistant director of outreach and athletics at Northeast Passage, a center for therapeutic recreation in Durham, New Hampshire, stated, "To play sled hockey, the only requirement is that you have a disability that prohibits you from playing stand up. That makes it very broad."

Sled hockey joined the Paralympics in the 1994 Norway Games. Team USA won the 2016 World Sled Hockey Challenge on Prince Edward Island, Canada. Thirteen of the players on that team joined the 2017–2018 U.S. National Sled Hockey Team, later taking their fourth straight title in the four-team event in December 2017, an unprecedented accomplishment, before moving on to the 2018 Winter Paralympics in South Korea, where they took gold.

Boarding the Snow

Snowboarding may have started when a father joined two skis for his daughter to "surf" the

Snowboarding Lesson from a Paralympian

During the California wildfires in October 2017, ten-year-old Lilly Biagini, a double amputee, and her mother lost everything in their house, including Lilly's prosthetic legs. Prior to the fire, Lilly had been walking independently for three years with the help of adjustable socket technology that enabled Lilly to control her own prosthetic socket fit by turning a dial. When the fire took away her prosthetics, it also took away her independence.

Lilly's prosthetic team from Hanger Clinic in California, SPS National Labs in Orlando, Florida, and manufacturers Endolite and College Park all worked together to produce new prosthetic legs for Lilly. Once back on her feet, Lilly got snowboarding lessons from US Paralympian and bronze medalist Keith Gabel. In an interview with ABC News, Gabel shared, "I've never met anybody with the spirit that Lilly has," and Lilly commented that being able to turn and stop independently made her "feel strong and proud."

slopes in the 1960s. By 2000, it was the nation's fastest-growing recreation. In spring 2017, 9.78 million people in the United States reported snow skiing or snowboarding in the past year. Who is a good candidate for adaptive snowboarding? People with body asymmetry may be especially

Amy Purdy, double amputee, adaptive snowboarder, and Paralympian, believes that having a disability allowed her to tap into her imagination and open herself up to all possibilities.

good candidates, such as those with cerebral palsy, amputations, spinal cord injuries, and hemiplegia, or paralysis of one side of the body. When going downhill, gravity is everyone's friend. And the terrain is the snowboarder's choice, from gentle slopes to steep areas not intended for ski runs.

Adaptive snowboarders can participate in different competitions, like the boardercross, full of turns, berms, obstacles, and jumps, and the slopestyle, a contest judged on tricks. Para snowboarding is enjoyed by athletes all over the world with various impairments, like impaired muscle ability, range of motion, or limb deficiency. Athletes are placed into one of three categories: two for leg impairments and one for arm impairments.

What happened when snowboarding debuted in the 2014 Sochi Paralympic Games? The United States dominated the men's snowboard-cross podium, and Amy Purdy took bronze for the women. If you want to get involved in adaptive snowboarding or other adaptive sports, check out Disabled Sports USA chapters or Paralympic Sport Clubs and hit the slopes!

10 Great Questions to Ask a Physical Therapist

1. How can I find the right adaptive sport for me?

2. How can I participate safely in adaptive sports?

3. Do I need to be evaluated to play adaptive sports?

4. What kind of modifications do I need to play?

5. What benefits will I enjoy from playing adaptive sports?

6. Are there local organizations where I can sign up to play?

7. Am I best suited for a team or individual sport?

8. What skills have I learned in physical therapy that would help me participate in sports?

9. How should I train for my sport?

10. What warning signs indicate that I am putting too much strain on my body?

Chapter Five

So Many Choices

If the adaptive sports already mentioned are not your thing, there are even more to choose from! Maybe shooting an arrow at the bullseye with archery is more your style? Or cycling in the great outdoors? What about mountain biking in rough terrain? Warm weather may make you think about getting in the water: surfing the waves, scuba diving, water skiing, or going rafting. Some people may prefer a leisurely ride on a horse or jumping hurdles in a competition. Think martial arts or tai chi sounds fun? Or maybe yoga is more your speed. Are you getting the picture? There is at least one sport out there for everyone—or even a combination of activities, like triathlons. So go for it!

Choose Your Ride

When you ride a bicycle, you can enjoy the outdoors, talk to other cyclists, and get a low-impact cardio, or heart, workout. While biking, cyclists also improve their coordination, strength, and balance. If you're interested in biking, it all begins with choosing the right bike. If your lower limbs are impaired, then handcycles allow cyclists to use their upper body strength to ride a three-wheeled bike. If you have visual impairments, then try a two-wheeled bike with a guide.

Balance challenges? Recumbent cycles are lower to the ground and come in different versions—like the tadpole—one wheel in back, two in front—and the delta, with two wheels

Since its development in the eighties, handcycling has become increasingly popular, with thousands of people taking part in the sport today.

in back and one in front. These bikes are also good for those with limited, or no, use of their lower body, such as people with cerebral palsy or neurological back injuries or those recovering from strokes. Other modifications, like those on the bike of an arm amputee that has the shifters and brake levers located on the side she has use of, may also be helpful. And don't forget to wear a helmet and eye protection.

Mountain biking takes cycling to a different level—the high-speed and exciting level! For example, people with disabilities can visit New England Disabled Sports at Bretton Woods in New Hampshire and take a ride on the ski lift, with bike in tow, and ride down Mount Washington. Sports director for New England Disabled Sports and paraplegic Geoff Krill says, "Mountain biking is just like alpine skiing, with different levels of trails. You can have a nice downhill ride or go as fast as you want to go. It's open to lots

No Olympic Counterpart

Competitors with cerebral palsy are among the most popular Paralympic boccia players, a game that also includes athletes with other impairments affecting their motor skills. Boccia consists of a white target ball called the jack. By throwing or rolling their colored balls, players try to get closest to the jack. The competitor or team with their ball closest to the jack earns a point. Any other balls of the same side that are closer than the opponents' also earns that team points.

Boccia is one of two Paralympic sports that does not have a counterpart in the Olympics. The other is goalball. Goalball is only for the blind or visually impaired. Six-player teams aim to score by throwing balls into a net while opponents try to stop them. Goalball debuted at the 1976 Toronto Paralympics.

of disabilities from amputees to quads." Anyone interested in mountain biking can make an appointment at a place that offers adaptive biking and talk about the kind of bike needed and what the ride feels like.

Mounting the Horse

Riding a horse has many benefits. Therapeutic riding, also known as hippotherapy, can have particular benefits for people with disabilities. Nicole Budden, founder and director of Happy Trails Riding Center in Oregon, maintains that "horseback riding is naturally therapeutic. Whether they have physical, cognitive, sensory or emotional dis-abilities, participants, such as those with cerebral palsy, benefit from riding or work-ing with horses." The horse-back riding experience can also include guidance on how to behave around horses and even how to groom them.

Hippotherapy uses the movement of horses as part of physical, occupational, or speech therapy to achieve goals such as increased muscle tone or decreased anxiety.

Horseback riding has phys-ical, cognitive, behavioral, and social benefits, including improved posture and muscle strength, better range of motion, better head and trunk control, and opportunities to practice under-standing both single-step and multistep directions. Riding a horse provides proprioceptive input—giving riders a sense of where their bodies are relative to space—and vestibular input, which registers move-ment and its speed.

Just being around horses puts people, including those with disabilities, in touch with other riders and instructors, increasing their opportunities for social interaction, as well as helping participants develop a healthy respect for animals. Many options

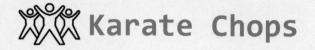 Karate Chops

Judo is a Paralympic sport only for visually impaired participants. The Paralympics has three different judo classes; each class divides athletes by weight. Paralympic judo is a lot like Olympic judo. Men compete for five minutes; women for four. Points are scored with attacks or getting opponents on the ground unable to move or compete further.

Another martial art, tae kwon do, is also a Paralympic sport. But this sport is open for participants with different impairments—like those with arm amputations. There are different styles of this martial art—with a form called Kyorugi, or sparring that involves techniques like kicking and blocking, as the main format set to appear in the 2020 Paralympics in Tokyo.

for adaptive horseback riding exist throughout the country, and many physical therapists can make recommendations.

Horseback riding, or equestrian, became a Paralympic sport in the 1996 Atlanta games. Participants can have physical or visual impairments. Competitions range from set movements to freestyle contests with music, with judges assessing skills. There are five classifications, from least to most severe disabilities.

Leibovitz wins Paralympic Gold in Table Tennis

Teenager Tahl Leibovitz was once homeless. His parents, who suffered from addiction and mental illness, threw Leibovitz out of the home at age thirteen—leaving him to live on the streets. Leibovitz eventually found the South Queens Boys and Girls Club, which helped at-risk youth and was introduced to table tennis. Still without a home, young Leibovitz played table tennis during the day and slept on the subway trains at night.

Meeting the coach of the U.S Paralympic Table Tennis Team changed Leibovitz's life. Leibovitz learned that he had osteochondroma, abnormal growth of cartilage and bone occurring near the end of the bone, which made him able to compete in the Paralympics. By 1996, Leibovitz won Paralympic gold for table tennis at the Atlanta games.

Eventually, Leibovitz achieved success in academics, too. He took the GED exam to obtain his high school diploma and earned two bachelor's degrees, in sociology and philosophy—and then two master's degrees, in urban affairs and social work. With the help of the USOC's Athlete Career and Education Program, which helps athletes with other aspects of life besides sports, Leibovitz began working as a substance abuse counselor.

In a Paralympic Team USA article, Angel Bovee, an athlete career and education career coach for disabled athletes, shared, "We always try to sell the

(continued on the next page)

(continued from the previous page)

fact that athletes are top performers in their sport, but they can also be top performers in the workplace. The soft skills they have—determination, problem-solving skills, teamwork mentality—that make them successful in sport are the very same skills that will make them successful in a job."

After participating in the 2016 Paralympics, Thal Leibovitz, shown here, stated that he hoped to continue playing competitive table tennis for eight more years.

For example, a classification of Grade 1b can include participants who are paralyzed from the waist down. One such rider is Hope Hand, former Paralympian and executive director of the U.S. Para-Equestrian Association (USPEA), who competed in the 2000 games with modifications, like two whips, stirrups with rubber bands, and a pommel with a strap. And Grades III and IV have riders who can walk without support, like Keith Newerla, 2004 National Para-Equestrian Trials grand champion, who competed using an adaptive saddle.

Paralympic Participation

Disabled athletes who want to participate in the Paralympics can try the activities discussed or compete in other sports currently included in the games or those that may be part of the Paralympics in the future, such as surfing.

Para archery is open to people with physical impairments and uses certain assistive devices to shoot the arrows. Para archery was the first sport to offer an organized competition for wheelchair participants. Another sport offered is wheelchair rugby, which is a combination of traditional rugby, handball, and basketball. Wheelchair rugby uses special wheelchairs designed for the sport. Rugby athletes have a variety of impairments involving their arms and legs, from limited functioning to paralysis.

Some athletes might want to try para table tennis. By number of athletes participating in a sport, table tennis is the third most popular, with more than forty million players participating in competitions. Players have different physical impairments other than visual impairments.

What if an athlete wants to do a combination of sports all in one competition? He or she might try a triathlon, which consists of swimming for 750 meters (820 yards), cycling for 20 kilometers (12.4 miles), and then running for 5 kilometers (3.1 miles). Classifications are based on physical impairments, with this sport happening in thirty-seven countries.

The Paralympic Games is just one venue for people with disabilities to participate in at least twenty sports. There are other places to get exercise and have fun with adaptive sports, too, like certain sports clubs, outdoor adventure programs, and physical education courses. Opportunities for people with disabilities to practice sports with modifications exist—so get involved!

Glossary

accessible Easily reached, used, or entered.

adaptive Able to adjust to different conditions.

amputee A person who has had a limb surgically removed.

cerebral palsy A condition caused by damage to the brain before or at birth that results in disabilities.

classifier Someone who determines which group athletes compete in.

cognitive Relating to the thinking processes of perception, memory, and judgment.

coordination Able to effectively use different parts of the body together.

hormone A chemical substance that occurs naturally in your body and controls and regulates specific cells or organs.

impairment The state of being weakened or diminished as it relates to one's ability to function.

inclusion The act of including someone or something as part of a larger group.

mobility Able to move, especially without much difficulty.

modification The act of changing something in a limited way to make it more useful for a certain population.

Paralympics International contests for athletes with disabilities that run parallel to the Olympic Games.

paraplegia Partial or full paralysis of the legs and

lower body, while maintaining the use of arms and legs.

prostheses Artificial devices that replace an impaired or missing limb.

recreational Relating to something done for fun or to relax.

rehabilitation Activities done to restore a physical condition by use of means such as physical therapy.

spinal cord The cord of nervous tissue that runs from the brain along the back in the spinal canal.

trunk A body part that does not contain the head or limbs.

veteran A person who has served in the armed forces.

For More Information

Adaptive Adventures
1315 Nelson Street, Unit 1
Lakewood, CO 80215
(303) 679-2770
Website: https://adaptiveadventures.org
Facebook and Instagram: @adaptiveadventures
Adaptive Adventures gives children and adults with
disabilities opportunities to participate in sports
such as cycling, climbing, kayaking, and rafting.

Adaptive Sports Foundation (ASF)
549 Chemin Knowlton
Knowlton, QC J0E 1V0
Canada
(450) 243-5985
Website: http://adaptivesports.ca
Facebook: @asfwindham
Instagram: @adaptive_sports_foundation
Twitter: @AdaptiveSportsF
YouTube: @adaptivesports
Adaptive Sports Foundation offers adaptive outdoor
sports opportunities tailored to the needs of indi-
viduals with physical disabilities.

Canadian Paralympic Committee
85 Plymouth Street, Suite 100
Ottawa, ON K1S 3E2
Canada
(613) 569-4333
Website: http://www.paralympic.ca

Facebook and Twitter: @CDNParalympics
Instagram: @cdnparalympics
The Canadian Paralympic Committee consists of
  twenty-five member organizations aimed at
  helping Canadian athletes participate and succeed
  in the Paralympic Games.

Disabled Sports USA
451 Hungerford Drive, Suite 608
Rockville, MD 20850
(301) 217-0960
Website: https://www.disabledsportsusa.org
Facebook: @DisabledSportsUSA
Twitter: @disabledsportus
YouTube: @DisabledSportsUS
Disabled Sports USA provides opportunities for indi-
  viduals with disabilities to participate in commu-
  nity sports, educational programs, and recreation.
  With chapters in more than forty states, Disabled
  Sports USA helps to improve the lives of youth
  and adults with disabilities in many communities.

US Paralympics
Division of United States Olympic Committee (USOC)
One Olympic Plaza
Colorado Springs, CO 80909
(888) 222-2313
Website: https://www.teamusa.org/us-paralympics
Facebook, Twitter, and Instagram: @USParalympics
The U.S. Paralympics supports athletes with
  Paralympic-eligible impairments.

For Further Reading

Alexander, Timothy, and Tim Stephens. *Ever Faithful, Ever Loyal: The Timothy Alexander Story.* Schererville, IN: Hilltop30 Publishers, 2018.

Birnbaum, Josh, and Matthew E. Buchi. *Dream Shot: The Journey to a Wheelchair Basketball National Championship.* Champaign, IL: The University of Illinois Press, 2017.

Brittain, Ian. *The Paralympic Games Explained.* Abingdon, United Kingdom: Routledge, 2016.

Civin, Todd, Dick Hoyt, and Rick Hoyt. *One Letter at a Time.* Herndon, VA: Mascot Books, 2012.

Cunningham, Ricardo A. *Adaptive Sports Fundamentals: A Step-by-Step Guide for Teaching Children and Young Adults the Fundamental Skills of 10 of the Most Popular Sports.* Seattle, WA: CreateSpace Independent Publishing Platform, 2016.

Davis, Lennard J. *Enabling Acts: The Hidden Story of How the Americans with Disabilities Act Gave the Largest US Minority Its Rights.* Boston, MA: Beacon Press, 2015.

Downing, Tricia. *Cycle of Hope: A Journey from Paralysis to Possibility.* Denver, CO: Front Street Press, 2017.

Long, Jessica. *Unsinkable: From Russian Orphan to Paralympic Swimming World Champion.* New York, NY: HMH Books for Young Reader, 2018.

Lyon, Drew. *Against All Odds* (Sports Illustrated Kids: Real Heroes of Sports). North Mankato, MN: Capstone Press, 2017.

Bibliography

ADA Tenth Anniversary. "Faces of the ADA." Retrieved February 2018. https://www.ada.gov/fmartin.htm.

American Physical Therapy Association. "Adaptive Sports: Staying Active While Living with a Disability." American Physical Therapy Association. Retrieved January 2018. https://www.moveforwardpt.com/Resources /Detail/adaptive-sports-people-with-disabilities.

Bragg, Beth. "Palmer Teen Makes Paralympics Nordic Ski Team." *Anchorage Daily News*, February 2, 2018. https://www.adn.com/sports /skiing/2018/02/01 /palmer-teen-makes-paralympic-nordic-ski-team.

Combs, Adam. Interview, Waypoint Adventure. Boston, Massachusetts, February 15 and 21, 2018.

Daniels, Mary. "Saddle Modifications for Para Equestrians." *Dressage Today*, June 20, 2010. https://dressagetoday.com/instructon/saddle _modifications_para_equestrians_062010-12417.

Disabled Sports USA. "Adaptive Sports." Retrieved January 2018. http://www.disabledsportsusa .org/sports/adaptive-sports.

Ewing, Sarah. "Ellie Simmonds: My Family Values." *The Guardian*, September 5, 2014. https://www.theguardian.com/lifeandstyle/2014 /sep/05/ellie-simmonds-my-family-values.

Gallagher, Sophie. "Rio Paralympics 2016: 9 Inspiring Quotes from Team GB Paralympians." *Huffington Post* (UK Edition), June 2016. http://www.huffingtonpost.co.uk/entry/inspiring

-quotes-team-gb-paralympics-2016_uk
_57cebe03e4b09f5b5e37b36d.

Hanger Clinic. "Empowered Stories: Lilly Biagini."
Retrieved February 2018. http://www
.hangerclinic.com/empowered-stories/Pages
/Lilly_Biagini.aspx.

Health24. "Benefits of Sport for People
with Disabilities." Retrieved January 2018. https://
www.health24.com/Fitness/Exercise/Benefits-of
-sport-for-people-with-disabilities-20130531.

International Paralympic Committee (IPC). "The
PyeongChang 2018 Paralympic Winter Games."
Retrieved January 2018. https://www.paralympic
.org.

Kelleher, Susan. "Seattle's Footloose Sailing Club:
'Leave Your Disability at the Dock.'" *Seattle Times*.
June 3, 2017. Retrieved March 2018. https://www
.seattletimes.com/seattle-news/seattle-sailing-club
-leave-your-disability-at-the-dock.

Kindelan, Katie. "10-year-old double amputee who
lost everything in California wildfires gets snowboard lessons from US Paralympian." ABC News,
December 12, 2017. http://abcnews.go.com
/Lifestyle/10-year-double-amputee-lost-california
-wildfires-snowboard/story?id=51586481.

Kiuppis, Florian. "Inclusion in Sport: Disability and
Participation." *Sport in Society*, Volume 21, Issue
1. August 30, 2016.

Maconi, Caryn. "Once a Homeless Teenager, Paralym-
pian Tahl Leibovitz Embraces New Career in Social
Work While Training for Rio." U.S. Paralympics,
March 1, 2016. https://www.teamusa.org
/US-Paralympics/Features/2016/March/01/Once

-homeless-Paralympian-Tahl-Leibovitz-embraces
-new-social-work-career-while-training-for-Rio.

Minnesota Public Radio News. "Personal Stories of the ADA's Impact." July 2010. https://www
.mprnews.org/story/2010/07/22/ada-stories.

National Institutes of Health: Eunice Kennedy Shriver National Institute of Child Health and Human Development. "How Many People Use Assistive Devices?" Retrieved January 2018. https://www
.nichd.nih.gov/health/topics/rehabtech
/conditioninfo/people.

Office of the Surgeon General. *The Surgeon General's Call to Action to Improve the Health and Wellness of Persons with Disabilities.* Retrieved February 2018. https://www.ncbi.nlm.nih.gov/books
/NBK44662.

Orr, James. "Who Is Ellie Simmonds? Paralympic Champion Swimmer Who's Won Five Gold Medals." *The Sun*, January 19, 2018. https://www
.thesun.co.uk/sport/3737540/ellie-simmonds
-paralympic-swimmer-five-gold-medals.

Special Olympics. "Special Olympics and Paralym-pics." Retrieved February 2018. http://media
.specialolympics.org/soi/files/press-kit/SO
-andPARALYMPICS_2014_FactSheet_Final.pdf.

Team Hoyt. "About Team Hoyt." Retrieved January 2018. http://www.teamhoyt.com/About-Team
-Hoyt.html.

U.S. Department of Veterans Affairs. "Paralympic Pro-gram Motivates Disabled Veterans." Retrieved Feb-ruary 2018. https://www.va.gov/health
/NewsFeatures/20120709a.asp.

Index

A

Americans with Disabilities Act (ADA), 4, 12, 14, 18
amputees, 4, 16, 23, 42, 47–48
archery, para, 44, 53
autism spectrum disorders, 4, 29

B

balance, 11, 38, 39, 46
  challenges to, 47
basketball, wheelchair, 6, 19–21, 27, 53
bones, 9, 51
  disease, 11–12
brain, 4, 9, 12

C

cerebral palsy, 4, 16, 29, 30, 38, 43–44, 47, 49
classifications, 16, 17, 30–31, 50, 52, 53
coordination, 11, 46
cycling, 10, 46–47, 53

D

Down syndrome, 4, 11–12, 29

E

exercise, 53
  benefits of, 4, 8–12, 13–15, 19

F

fencing, wheelchair, 19, 23

H

heart, 9, 10, 46
  disease, 11
hockey, sled, 22, 37, 40, 42
hormones, 4, 9, 13
horseback riding, 46, 48–50
Hoyt, Rick, 25, 26

I

Individuals with Disabilities Education Act (IDEA), 11, 12, 18
impairments
  arm, 39, 44, 53
  hearing, 38
  intellectual, 6, 29, 31, 37, 38
  leg and feet, 28, 39, 44, 53
  neurological, 30
  physical, 4, 6, 29, 31, 37, 44, 50, 53
  visual, 24, 29, 30, 31, 38, 39, 47, 50, 53

L

Leibovitz, Tahl, 51
Long, Jessica, 31
lungs, 9

M

martial arts, 46, 50
Martin, Casey, 14
Miller, Grace, 41
mobility, 19
  impairment, 24–25

modifications, 4, 6, 15, 29, 31, 33, 34, 37-38, 47, 52, 53
muscles, 4, 9, 11
muscular system, 9, 10, 29

N
nerves, 9
nervous system, 9

P
paddle sports, 29-31, 36
paraplegia, 29, 37, 47
  requirements to compete, 17
prostheses, 24, 31

R
rehabilitation program, 20, 40
running, 19, 24, 26, 53
  visually impaired, 16

S
sailing, 29, 33-34
Simmonds, Ellie, 32
skiing, 6, 29, 39, 42-43, 44, 47
  cross-country, 37, 38, 39
  downhill, 37, 38, 39
  equipment, 15-16, 34, 36
  programs, 37-38
  sit, 34, 37, 38-39
  two-track, 38
  water, 34, 36, 46
snowboarding, 37, 42-43, 44
Special Olympics, 6, 16-17, 18
spina bifida, 29, 42
spinal cord, 9

  injuries to, 42, 43-44
stretching, 11
swimming, 9, 10, 29, 31, 32, 53

T
table tennis, para, 6, 51, 53
tennis, 19
  wheelchair, 27
triathlon, 26, 46, 53
trunk, 28, 30
  balance, 39
  control, 49

V
veterans, 21-22
  World War II, 20
volleyball, 6, 19, 27
  sitting, 22-23

W
Waypoint Adventure, 35-36
Wheelchair Basketball Federation, 19
wheelchairs, 10, 15-16, 19, 20, 21, 25, 27, 28, 30, 31, 36, 39
  accessibility, 23
  archery, 53
  basketball, 19, 20-21
  dancers, 6
  fencing, 28
  push-rim, 24-25
  ramps, 4
  rugby, 53
  sports, 19
  tennis, 27

About the Author

Barbara Gottfried is the author of numerous books. She has participated in several textbook projects with Pearson Education, in the areas of interpersonal studies and life skills. As the parent of a son with severe cerebral palsy, Gottfried and her family have participated in many events with both Yachad and Friendship Circle. Gottfried holds a BA from the University of Michigan and an MA from New York University, specializing in statistics and econometrics.

Photo Credits

Cover, p. 1 Santypan/Shutterstock.com; p. 5 Jeff Greenberg/Photolibrary/Getty Images; p. 7 Splash News/Alamy Stock Photo; p. 10 Maskot/Getty Images; p. 13 Joe Giddens-EMPICS/PA Images/ Getty Images; p. 15 David Maxwell/AFP/Getty Images; p. 16 Kyodo News/Getty Images; p. 20 AFP/Getty Images; pp. 22, 30, 34 © AP Images; pp. 26, 42 Boston Globe/Getty Images; p. 27 ZUMA Press, Inc./Alamy Stock Photo; p. 31 Buda Mendes/ Getty Images; pp. 33, 40 Tim Clayton/Corbis/Getty Images; p. 38 Wolfgang Kaehler/LightRocket/Getty Images; p. 44 Matthew Stockman/Getty Images; p. 47 Shahjehan/Shutterstock.com; p. 49 Anton Novoderezhkin/TASS/Getty Images; p. 52 Ben Gabbe/Getty Images.

Design: Tahara Anderson; Editor: Jennifer Landau; Photo Researcher: Sherri Jackson